In the Blink of a Mottled Eye

In the Blink of a Mottled Eye

Poems by

Michelle Reale

Cover design by Shay Culligan

ISBN: 978-1-950462-95-7

Kelsay Books Inc.

kelsaybooks.com

502 S 1040 E, A119
American Fork, Utah 84003

Dedicated to those I love

Acknowledgments

Grateful acknowledgment is given to the following publications for previous publication of some of these poems: *Thickjam, Thrush, Dogzplots, Menacing Hedge, Anti-Heroin Chic, Word Fountain Review, Mom Egg Review* and *Italian-Americana.*

Contents

The Things that never
Can come back, are
several—
Childhood—some
forms of Hope—the
Dead.

—Emily Dickinson, #1515

Passed years seem safe ones, vanquished ones, while the future
lives in a cloud, formidable from a distance.

—Beryl Markham, *West with the Night*

The days aren't discarded or collected, they are bees
that burned with sweetness or maddened
the sting: the struggle continues,
the journeys go and come between honey and pain.

—Pablo Neruda, *Still Another Day*

Equidae

Not all theories
are prescriptive. Getting
through the day

is a spiritual act,
the blue and yellow
lessons it taught me

nearly always forgotten
by the weekend. I shoved
green in the corner and stalked

the pink horse all the way
to its natural border where
it could hang its heavy head

and sway on fragile legs. I marked x's
in strategic places. I hoped to find my way
back, if only I had memory to

begin again. The happiness will
come either before or after
the sadness leaves me bereft

at the falling fence, but I
am not taking sides. An accelerant
with just the right ignition

will catch fire
in all the right places
because it is in its nature to do so.

My Mother Kneels

My mother kneels on the floor by the chair where I sit, my legs straight like poles. My hand in hers, she folds down two fingers to reveal three. My age. She smiles. I reach for the cobwebs in her hair and she slaps my hand into a lap of cookie crumbs. When I am five, my mother holds her hand up to me and all five fingers wave like a banner in praise of my existence. I am in command of myself that year as she hands me a flashlight. I crouch beside her and shine the light on her dimpled thigh. She holds the worn handle of a paring knife, and filets a chunk of wood from beneath her skin. She swabs the area with carmine red, winces at the sting. I think the source of her pain is chemical. This was the year a dog, who was not ours, barked all night. The year I woke in the middle of the night to a mild earthquake, folding our walls like an accordion. I stood in the dark of my parents' bedroom where they told me to go back to bed, to never mind what I felt. My lips were sealed against the telling. The wind blew and blew and blew.

Learning Curve

To claim the affection of someone who you pretend is dead is to be loved into perpetuity. I've lost so many layers over time and I made the recommended changes long ago.

Newsprint fingers are a thing of the past and for all I care, world events can float through me like the radiation from our first color television set that my father wheeled proudly through our front door on the old wooden dolly.

My brother told me everyone wore green makeup on TV, a lie I inexplicably still believe. Then, like now, Technicolor and dimensionality mesmerized me.

When I first met you I thought the broad base of your feet were a bought and signed for foundation to the future and then I learned how much legroom a normal-sized person is allotted on a Greyhound bus with a one-way ticket.

I was the best black sheep in the family, all Peter Pan collars, sensible shoes and wishful thinking. I was jealous of deferential women who cleaned the fingernail dust behind them, and those who desired nothing more than collecting decorative rocks for the homemade grotto, a place for radical worship and feverish sacrifice. A few years ago, the honeymoon resort turned out their 40-watt bulbs,

drained the diseased heart-shaped tubs and padlocked the pine-knotted doors. It was a place that reminded me of all of the weather phenomena of my youth: a lot of hullabaloo and empty promises. The currents of wind notwithstanding, the plaster of Paris Virgin Mary hums the first tonal bars of the Ave Maria, and the red fox that roams the neighborhood ovulates under the full moon.

I ask for all the wrong things when I pray. I break a tablet in pieces. Sleep with one half under my pillow where all my wishes are dying stars. The other under my serrated edged tongue. Wake when I blink. *Kiss me anyway.*

This Year my Sorrow Drowns Itself

This year my sorrow drowns itself. I can't be responsible anymore.
Here is where I'm at: you've nailed my hair to the floorboards, and
I lay

quiet, all shallow breathing like certain death. You claim to see the
shadow of a dowager's hump and fiddle with a fragile bone at the
base

of my neck. You predicted a distance between us while you filled
the air with the ghosts of other bodies you have seen, those you
have feigned

affection for. Was it a dream when you claimed extreme
deficiency, ugliness in the body that housed your un-children? I
might have

imagined or maybe I just like to pretend. My long arms circle my
broad waist while my mirror image quells your hard edge; let the
blood

do a decent job, and clot, once and for all. I am displacement here
and no longer take any vows I can't rescind with the blink of my
mottled

eye. All familiar settings deny me the gloss of the finish that
belongs to me. It is what we have all been waiting for. At the
ancestral level, I am

grateful for inheritance. At the collective level, I whisper remedies
and white doves that whisper urgencies of lost love. You will wait
me out.

This body. This temple. These peonies decorate the transformation of all the fables I have knitted in my pale hands. And still, I cannot, without

the distortion of the eternally optimistic, make my prayers heard over the sharp-edged bone.

Post Traumatic

My brother comes home from school where he tells me he learns about the world. I sit Indian-style on the floor next to him with a pencil and paper. *Alphabetical,* I say to him because it is my favorite word. This was while I was still precocious. My mother is swabbing the kitchen floor with Spic 'n Span and the lollipop in my mouth begins to taste the way it smells: clean and grainy. *History homework now,* my methodical brother says. He glances at our new Philco console television, our pride and joy. Walter Cronkite, neatly framed, narrates the unreal. Men with bare chests where dog tags lay, smoke cigarettes hanging from their lips, their faces smeared, dark and scary. The sweat, the smoking, the shooting. *Enemy territory,* Cronkite growls. My mother drops her mop and angrily twists the dial off, but I have already seen. I draw a face on the page with large eyes, and a mouth like a like a gash from ear to ear. My brother opens his mouth to speak, but no sound comes out.

I Dreamt I Was the Moon

 I watched dilapidation encroach, foolishly engaged in utopian thinking—it seemed to have worked for others. My own porous bones were no match for the yellowed linoleum, curling away from the corners that it used to fit into with perfection. The brindle cat, swollen with internal pockets of blood from blind outrage,the latest epidemic and without a cure. The dog like a sentry at the back door, awaiting not arrival, but escape. *Who belongs?* Every day another improvisation: coffee, a light meal, a heavy sigh, the balled fist, the washing up. In the gloaming we slept cracked to crooked spine, twisting in the bedrock of someone else's folktale. *Your fingertip in my eye for the presence of tears in the dark, an ongoing deficit that enraged.* Later, the cold bluish light of morning, like a ring of gas flame, extinguished my *belvedere.* Your lazy footsteps behind me, like you were tracking spoor. Predictably, and to your delight, I faltered. The strong, bitter coffee stewing in the glass, stovetop pot, became impatient. My gaze fixed at the medicinal sky, forever considered the threshold of forfeitures, blessed the smooth contours of silence that would allow me to get away with my life, one more time.

East Vineland, New Jersey, 1930

Genoa Avenue and an expanse as temporal as a bad memory. Jews
and Italians shudder in the

sun. *The cultivators. The scorned.* Everyone with a purpose. Even
the sister with the lame leg,

pushes her broom from one side to the other, dragging her heavy
shoe across the kitchen

floorboards until the ruts insure she makes her mark. The father
with his hand-rolled

cigarettes and his white, long-sleeved shirts made from altar cloth,
bludgeoning the dirt into the

submission his wife will not accept. Here is the brevity of
commitment. Here is purification by

all of the aseptic wonders of the world. In the potato house you
sleep one tender body next to

another, five to a bed. The Legion of Mary followers regularly
collapse and cry at the vision of

hell fire and deprivation while the Jews laughed like the
condemned they would be. The harvest

will be good every year, the fields the blessing of the undeserved.
An unfurling of misery. An unfurling

of mercy. A revenant who shows himself in the light of day. A
tincture for everyone afflicted in equal measure.

When Funds Fail to Meet Demands

The account binders on the shelf that I never had time for. Your ledger of forfeitures and on every line a minus sign. I see my name strategically placed or maybe I only think that I do. What you gave I used up, took away. Everything you ever wanted circled a drain already clogged with my thick hair, your desperation, my homesickness for a place I'd never been. The cheerfulness of the old wallpaper in the kitchen, a remnant of the previous owner, a woman who drank too much and wore a shade of lipstick unbecoming. I said it was an omen, you said it was just another symptom. We existed in our own echo chamber, the walls throbbing with our own desperate attempts. At your request I switched a small light over a carved Buddha every night. *My symbolic duty.* One piercing point of light cast a long shadow. The house shuddered. It was one single catastrophe: paradoxical in its precision. Devastating in how little remained.

Hurricane Agnes, 1972

A girl watches the rain fall. It is warm, but she has a prescient nature. Her arms are full of goosebumps. She gathers herself around her and is comforted by the woman in the house attached to theirs, who comes onto the porch, yanking up a tube top. The woman lights a cigarette, smokes like it might be her last, but exhales in disgust. She leaves when she hears the phone ringing inside, leaving the girl to watch the rain alone, but she wants her neighbor to come back, an ersatz mother. She thinks about her brother in his room. He hates rain. She thinks how unfortunate she can't swim and wonders if she would slide off the roof if she should need to take shelter there. She hears the neighbor in her house, her panicked voice betraying her defiant nerves of steel in face of the rising water level. *Don't call it a hurricane,* she hisses into the receiver, probably to her husband. She threatens her noisy kids with a tight slap if they all don't *shut up right now.* The girl's mother, stuck at work, calls, advises her to stay inside and don't drink the water: *tell your brother.* Finally, her brother comes out of his room and together, in the humid dampness, watch the water level rise. They hear sirens. The wrath of God, the nuns might say. I'm hungry her brother says, in his most take charge voice ever. They go inside and watch television with the sound turned up. Wait it out.

The Day Before She Died

she played Rock of Ages on the small organ that wheezed to life when we plugged it in. *Sounds like me,* she laughed, wiping a tear from the corner of her eye.

My brother ran the double reels of recording tape like a sound engineer while she played her songs, "Swanee River" (a favorite) and "Turkey in the Straw." I danced and hopped with energy around the room, tapping out of time

annoying everyone as usual. I remember her hands, so poised above the organ, which she held on her lap. Sometimes she closed her eyes and sometimes she pressed on the keys so hard, I thought they'd break.

After our lunch meat sandwiches were eaten and my grandmother nursed a cup of coffee, my brother played back the tape and we laughed and laughed at our voices, but my grandmother was proud

of the way she played our old favorites. My brother was so cool in his bell-bottom pants with the stripes and his U.S.A shirt like a banner when it was still cool to be patriotic.

He teased me about my hair: there's a horse somewhere who is missing a tail and my funny voice, calling me pipsqueak. My mother stood in the kitchen with my grandfather

both of them smoking a cigarette, and shouted *cut it out!* My little sister, still hearing the music in her own head twirled until she felt dizzy and fell down, fell right asleep where she landed.

That night, I vowed to learn the songs my grandmother knew by heart. She could teach me. These were some of the songs we sung at school, during music, which everyone hated, but that I loved so much.

The next day my mother thanked God that she and my father
bought the expensive tape recorder for my brother, the one they
resisted buying for so long.

That tape and hundreds of cigarettes kept
my mother company with a calendrical
rhythm like the weather.

Radicle

My small fingers broke the box-shaped dirt, revealing delicate, thread-like roots. My father knelt beside me. I pressed the orange marigold roots into the dirt he'd prepared. My father blessed himself, touched my forehead. Clouds moved across the sun while my father continued to dig. I had moved on to chalk the sidewalk, drawing arterial roots to somewhere in pastels the colors of Easter eggs. My father said I had cartography in my blood. When he held the crushed leaves of a marigold under my nose, I knew that somehow, we had breached arbitrary frontiers. *Smells like pepper, no?* He brushed the dirt from his knees and held his hand out to me. We smelled the garlic hitting the oil from my mother inside, at the stove. My father told me how roots were so fragile, how easily they can break. It took me years to understand. We held a willing suspension of belief as long as we could. Basked in the kind of radiance that came from the way we could console one another in the only language we knew.

Thick Jam

She decided to explain the pluot thus: not a peach, not a plum. Not your mother's jam. Like your favorite uncle wearing your aunt's polka dot dress.

Because he said he'd grown used to it, she would clarify the taste of brine, but none would be found in the vicinity. Instead she'd go on and on about the velvety consistency it had when spread on a fresh loaf.

Convince him that the reddish sweetness was something he could not live without, this man who she just slept with on crimson sheets, in a room she'd fashioned after what she envisioned Versailles to be.

The imagination can only take one so far. Now she would have to rip it all apart and start from scratch. He lay curled onto himself in the bed and felt a great shame in waking someone from such a deep sleep.

She'd phone a discreet friend instead and collect on a favor that had been gathering moss. So much depends on the ability to begin again. She'd lay the breakfast table with precision and toast the bread.

Lick the sweetness from her fingers. Leave the back door open. *Gallup into the yard and set those fruit bearing trees on fire.*

Deepfield

I don't remember if I took one last
look around or if I considered the life
of the plant that wept itself dry on the warped
windowsill and compared it to my own.

I didn't know years later that I would still
shamble in and out of every room, dragging my feet
through the gaping, blood-shot eye of the house, searching for a
mythic heritage.
*The counter balance to my straw man strategy was just me, all
flinty and agnostic.*

Once I stood by the light of the big picture window
admiring the bloom of a bruise so fresh; violet
and mottled, my arm delicately aloft, at waist level,
I tried so hard to erase blood memory, all my rough edges.

The world was so big all of a sudden, unbounded
by the constraints of sheetrock and temporality.
Galaxies were expanding though I thought of things in only two
ways:
Gasping for breath and *close to the edge.*

In the yard, the grass was so dry it hurt.
The shrub where the cat used to hide, from what
we will never know, leaned to the left. I was creating a corpus of
desire. Impermanence and the blue peony wallpaper mocked me at
every turn.

*Currents shift and I count nouns. I ask people questions.
I try to get back to thirsty and provisional.*

Dream Machine #1 Circa 1991

She wears a felt cap to bed when she ovulates. Her husband feels like he is sleeping with Celestine V. There is a sort of digital rhythm to their lovemaking, an explosion of corpuscles like a Rorschach test. The solfeggio thrums in the background, aiding the vibrational vortex, but mid-thrust and they lose their will. Populating the world is not a Roman holiday. They both long for the Prussian blue light that would invigorate the bravery they would need to get to the next step. A seedbed of truth would need to be tilled in the morning.

Dream Machine #2 Circa 1985

His manners were restrained, like a dog tugging on a leash. Her wore a faded military uniform, and made elaborate gestures of obeisance to all the wrong people. When they first met, she intuited a hidden charm, a secret he was hiding. He cooked dinner for her. Used his best bone china set, inherited from his mother, a woman who broke every rule for living right. It stirred something primitive in her. After dinner, she fondled his rusted buttons, massaged his drooping epaulets. Set her dish on the floor to let his piebald dog lick it clean.

There Might be Another Way of Saying This

I'd been in his house a week. I still didn't have a key. I missed my old place and wondered if it missed me, too. The night was a cold one. Windy, too. I imagined it was the windows and doors of my place, unoccupied for the foreseeable future, howling in grief, wondering when I would return. I used to think things like that. It was another life. He reached across the crumpled flannel sheets for me. I felt the weight of all of it. Crooked spine to crooked spine he slept. I stuttered in the darkness. I walked the foreign hallway and tried to and reached for a doorknob that was higher than it needed to be. I sought my own level, but I was out of fashion. I wanted to hold a steaming cup of something in my hands. *Anything that could penetrate layers.* He told me that my loneliness had a life cycle and that he would take care of it. *Just watch,* he said. My whole life I wanted to believe. Miracles were only coincidences, flinty things. My feet were so cold on that floor, but I welcomed it. I needed to *feel.* Leaning against the sink I felt his presences and turned to him. I wasn't guilty but I was no innocent, either. He flipped the kitchen light on and I was bathed in malignant yellow, my eyes watering. *Can't a girl think?* I snapped. I saw a shadow like an eclipse that comes once every hundred years pass over his unshaven face, that seemed to burn around the jaw. *Kidding!* I laughed. I held my steaming cup to him as an offering. He took it and turned his back.
Walked away from me.

The Stories I Told After the War

Were meant to entertain, not instruct. Still, I tried to convince. The laughing, like broken fingernails playing a ballad on a mandolin: you know what you hear but can't describe the sound. The body will blush under assault, but that is something felt, not necessarily seen and so won't hold up in a court of law. Men in suits claim they are trying to make progress for everyone, but I am still waiting. I am not everyone. I am not even me. The season that the orange fox roamed my neighborhood, I took it as a sign and warned the others. The constellations became faint and the few things left in my garden continued to grow, but underground. A generation of dead animal carcasses will never go hungry again. Above ground I spoke with the parched voice of the already damned, the mistrusted and ultimately forgotten. There were a lot of stories being told. In one, it was said that there are two types of people left after any military skirmish: The people who tell the truth about the oppressive regime that they've escaped, and the people left behind who lie to themselves in order to endure it. And everyone remains hungry, all the same.

Sedate

I am a calming cobalt blue. A contradiction. Really, I am a
problem solver, a gift from my mother. The ash she'd let grow so
long on her cigarette, I thought it would grow legs and walk away.
She had gifts like that. She'd survey the wisdom of the crowd and
make proclamations that people tended not to believe, but I did.
She kept keys around her neck, deprived of the proper locks. She'd
tell me, *free yourself.* Her name was so long, my imaginary friends
and I sang it like a chant, a tribute. The pink satin dress with the
rosette's accumulated dust along the shoulders. It looked so
dejected, month after month hanging as if an executioner stood
right behind. *Not yet,* she kept saying, though I longed to see the
shimmer on her form. Maybe it was real. A pin stuck in an
alternative universe, a thin membrane peeled back like banana
skin. My mother, in that pink satin dress, kneeling on a hardwood
floor. Somewhere, my father hummed a beer commercial bathed in
television glow. A knife in her hands and she digs a piece of wood
from her thigh. She stabs and stabs. There is no blood, just
splinters multiplying in the ruts of her skin. I hold the flashlight. I
do my part. *Here,* she hisses. *Over here, on me.* Almost, but not
quite.

Victorian Phraseology

Here is reinvention: If you don't like me, I can contort myself until you do. Pull my stays until I am blue in the face. Look my way. Hear me speak. I can unfurl my tongue to accommodate Victorian phraseology. The potential calisthenics of bodily organs give me hope today, but might worry me tomorrow. I am encouraged by the lift of your bushy brow. It makes me want to go further. I consider a colorful snood to match my eyes. Maybe peekaboo bangs, or eyebrows like Suzie Wong. I never claimed the innocence of intentions. I can think for myself. I am a crescendo in a minimalist orchestra where every note is a plaintive whine. You were here just a minute, an hour or a few years ago. I have street view maps but don't know where to begin. Are you lost? I know where I am. I am Theda Bara, heaving a heavy sigh on the railroad tracks, flapping my heavy Max Factor eyelashes. There is no simple cure. Trace the arterial routes of my thrombitic veins to a heart that has turned itself inside out. In another country they might call this a syndrome; in yet another, a disease. I call it a romantic myth. The important thing is that it is treatable. Do you smell my burning hair? Can you see the tiny flicker of flame in my ocular region? *Rescue me.*

Liberation Army

Well, you know, it's really been, you know, quite a trip for me.
—Patty Hearst

Everything pointed to survival. I was Patty Hearst with a loaded gun, but really, more like meringue: all flourish with little substance.

The cinnamon I craved was dark as peat, still, I sprinkled it over everything. My task was subjective. I tied the Gordian knot and focused on digestion.

The suppression of the lump in my throat was a collaborative effort. My peripheral vision has failed me more than once, my words concise in a clutch.

I used to live in a country where a broken heart was a sin, but then I crossed the border. The gentry invested in my doubt, waited for what I might

leave behind, then rifle through in my things. Consolation comes in the form of lies. If we could put our algorithms to better use, the government might treat us

like loyal children who only crave a warm glass of milk before bed. I am nearly pavlovic at the initial tonal hints of the Ave Maria. I weep into my princess

sleeves, but I remain strong enough to catch a dying star in my bare hands, a sure cure for persistent melancholy.

The man who beat his dog, lost his wife, but found her again. It is a love story I am fond of telling, though the optics are troubling.

My friends miss me so much. I once said soldier when I meant to say shoulder, conflating the weight of our extraordinary burdens and obligations, spread evenly among us.

Through the velvet fog we endure, but still we are impressed by the shelf life of everyday agonies. Utopian thinking has a purpose because the seasons are, after all
persistent.

Call me Tania.

Nihil Obstat

My grandmother was named for sorrow. White dimity cloth and a votive candle. She was unafraid of the dead who would gather at her feet or startle her when she was drinking her morning coffee. She'd admonish them for their departure, then pray to the Sacred Heart to take them away again. *Keep them where they belong. They have no place among the living.* She feared only her dreams, how they would tell not only the future, but the past, like sly whores with no shoes. The meals she cooked for her husband contained shortcuts, bitter herbs and resignation. Her rosary, well worn, hung on a hook next to her coat. Her heart turned in on itself, too tired for the explanations, years of successive novenas, his amber beer bottles, and her own face staring out at herself day after day from the chipped mirror in the cold bathroom on the second floor.

Say You Want a Revolution

One can't measure up to those who stay seated. Flick through the channels while they protest in the streets. Raise your fist in the air, swing it around a bit. If the revolution doesn't come around this time, surely, there will be other opportunities. Promise your loved ones the next time you won't dally; you'll be ready and among the crowds in your peaked cap. Give careful instructions to the ones who depend upon you. Tell your mother to light the stove. The couscous can wait. Tell your father it is useless to worry his beads. Bring your baby brother along, because hope cannot be learned soon enough. Let the bearded talking heads on *Al-Jezeera* broadcast to the room with the heavy curtains, to the chair, that will still be warm from where you nested, perhaps just moments before. The one that will be waiting your inevitable, dejected return.

Palermo

So many things can happen out of the country.
Take for instance the indecision inherent in choosing just one
flavor from a display of

gelato. I could be so simple, really, if the world would just let me.
I give instructions to newcomers.

Point to the flavor you like then ignore the roll of the eyes.
Hold out several inscrutable coins in the palm of your moist,
delicate hand.

Dare them to take what they want. Feign surprise when they do.
Lean over a wrought iron balcony and let your paper

serviette drift over the heads below, like an emissary of some
misbegotten peace.

Watch it stick to the shoe of a gentleman with no discernible place
to go. Chew with with your mouth open. Pretend not to understand.

Contemplate the vagaries that follow you wherever you might find
yourself. There is a baroque candlestick burning in an ancient
window.

It is not for you.

Dream Machine #3 Circa 1979

She liked to tell how she was wearing an Alice blue dress when she met the man of her dreams, a man with thick scars of loss. I imagined her an angry Alice in Wonderland, her short dress, with an incongruous short white apron. No, no she said, not that Alice. She became his sea siren, his savior. They were now two. *I am blue,* I said. They scolded my greedy indulgence; *see the world full of need?* She with her sly blue eyes, narrowed into derision. I fingered the little blue mark, where she jammed a number two pencil in to my thigh. *He's mine now,* she said. Be kind, he reminded her. He stared at the piece of lead I'd carried deep in the flesh, reaping hatred into muscle memory. In the mirror, I held my breath. A bluish tint bloomed on bloated lips. I thought it could be that easy. She stood behind me. She looked lovely in blue. The dress would be mine in due time. I would wear it when I was bold enough to steal something that should never belong to me in the first place. I'd make someone proud.

We the Women

We were six in that small place, and too many. Close enough together to smell derision. We were all tourists, though we pretended not to be. The woman with the green butterfly clipped in her hair hung on to her German husband. He squeezed her small breast for show then raised a small glass of dark beer our way. Winked. The men at our table laughed. Encouraged, he spoke: *In Egypt, a man offered four goats for my wife.* The artichokes came to the table. The men watched, we, the women, take sections into our mouths. I tongued my lips, looked sideways at the German. *Ah, she wants to play,* he said, forgetting himself. More than power shifted. The artichokes sat in their juices, glistening. My man placed a firm hand on my arm, and gripped. The blood rushed to my head. The German stood, lifted his small wife by her tiny arm. His embroidered serviette, pristine, fell to the sticky floor. The woman patted the butterfly in her hair. I looked for the powder on her fingers. There was none. The butterfly wasn't real, of course. *But, God, I wanted it to be.*

When in Rome

One hand under her skirt and another with an open palm toward
me. A slow shake of my head and her eyes flash. *No.* She knows
what she

wants, walks steady in my direction. She spits a gob in disgust,
smiles when I flinch. Crosses herself and rolls her eyes into the
back

of her head, cackles. The balcony above me holds a plaster
Madonna, thick vines choking her lily white neck, a crushed
cigarette pack at her

feet, foil all glittery and promising. There were one or two things I
used to know about this city, but God, the heat, in the evenings and

everything disappears. I sleep with the stone weight of the dead
hear the hiss of *caritas* like an ancient lullaby. What remains is
everything I have tried to forget:

Razor wire smile and a gold tooth.

Dream Machine #4 Circa 2019

My mother gave me bad news in between cracking eggs on the side of her new non-stick frying pan. *I wanted to voice a regret,* but she held up a hand, said we don't speak the same language. I saw the downcast eyes. I felt the blood jet like a brooding benediction. I'd felt my father's emotional spasms for years, the festering depths of what can never be cured. I've tripped down every dark corridor, laced my fingers through the religion of my ancestors and still cannot occupy liturgical space. Scar tissue is thick and the demarcation line has faded. I pulled gold filament through my gapped teeth, and drank a tea of nettles. My grandfather reinforced the retaining walls while all our forgotten cousins hurled their broken bodies in our direction, digging their dirty nails into our forearms. *Eat,* my mother commands, pushing the plate toward me. *The epidemic will arrive any moment.* The blind dog barks into stark nothingness.

In the Blink of a Mottled Eye

We embrace the role of the grateful chorus.

      We band together in a time of buds and rumors of buds
on trees, forget what haunts,

taunts and terrifies.

      Now you see it, now you don't.

Memory can raise the temperature of the room. Time a prolepsis:
everything ahead of us.

      Step away from the hour. Let us unfurl our taught bodies
into the tic of infinite

minutes.

About the Author

Michelle Reale is a professor at Arcadia University. She is the author of six academic books in her field of librarianship and the author of eleven collections of poetry. Forthcoming in 2019 is *Confini: Poems of African Refugees in Sicily* (Cervena Barva Press). Reale is the Founding and Managing editor *of Ovunque Siamo: New Italian-American Writing* and has twice been nominated for a Pushcart Prize.

www.ingramcontent.com/pod-product-compliance
Lightning Source LLC
Chambersburg PA
CBHW031154090426
42738CB00008B/1328